RADICALLY SIMPLE
TRAINING

Pro Tips and Strategies for
Exceptional Speakers and Trainers

TAMI SHAW
edited by **Joe Shaw**

Radically Simple Training
Copyright © 2025 by Tami Shaw

All rights reserved. No part of this book may be reproduced, distributed, or transmitted in any form or by any means, including photocopying, recording, or other electronic or mechanical methods, without the prior written permission of the publisher or author, except in the case of brief quotations embedded in critical reviews or articles.

Positive Strategery
www.PositiveStrategery.com

Editing By: Joe Shaw
Interior Format: Paul Nomshan

ISBN: 979-8-9927241-0-3 (paperback)

You know that feeling when you're *stuck* in a training that's *ugh*... such a misuse of your time?

We've all experienced it, so why does it continue to happen? Why are there so many mediocre trainings?

The root cause is often the trainer or speaker's overconfidence in their own ability to teach the content, their energy or style, or ineffective preparation. Whatever the reason... it's preventable.

When you're called to share your story and experiences, to teach and speak in order to help others grow, you want to be *exceptional* at it. And great news- you don't need a degree in training; you just need some radically simple tips and strategies.

Ready to become exceptional?

CONTENTS

Part 1: Best Book Intro Activity Ever 7
Part 2: Essential Trainer Beliefs 13
Part 3: Plan Like A Pro 35
Part 4: Start Strong 51
Part 5: End Strong 67
Part 6: Make It Memorable 77
Part 7: Discussions & Groups 83
Part 8: Breaks & Movement 105
Part 9: Improv Games With Meaning 117
Part 10: Call Backs & Attention Signals 131
Part 11: Choose Your Words 139
Part 12: Tips for Facilitating a Virtual Training 151
Part 13: Rad Simple Ways to Keep Improving 159
Credits & Bonus Resources 169

Part 1

Best Book Intro Activity Ever

Your Training
Pro Tips

You've likely attended workshops and conferences. You've heard keynote speeches, panels, and presentations. Before I share *my* radically simple tips, let's take a few minutes to tap into *your* experiences.

Create two sections on a piece of paper: one for "Greatness Elements" and one for "Pet Peeves." (There's a page for you in the Appendix, so your ideas can literally become part of this book.)

Let's start with Greatness Elements. What do you remember about your favorite workshops and speeches? Think of specifics.

For me, four unique talks come to mind where the speaker wrote a simple diagram on a giant poster paper on stage. Years later, I can tell you their main point and what they drew on the poster. When it comes to workshops, I rarely remember the presentation; my Greatness Elements include specific interactive experiences and rich discussions. Also on my personal list of Greatness Elements are memorable stories tied to a deep message. As an example, I'll never forget when I heard a story about how standing your ground against a goose is a hilarious and gut-wrenching metaphor for leadership… that even when you do all the right things, sometimes you still get beat up.

What's on *your* Greatness Elements list? Be specific about what you remember that made it great, such as the trainer's energy, a mantra, a joke, a visual, a discussion prompt, or an interactive experience. **Ponder your experiences, then make your list.**

Next, **jot down your Pet Peeves.** We can learn as much from the poor examples as the great ones. Consider what drives you bonkers in workshops or talks. What makes you think: *Ugh. Bleh. It's the worst when… I wish they didn't…*

My Pet Peeves list includes the speaker or trainer starting with their resume or family pictures, doing cheesy icebreakers, and going over time at the end of a full day.

How about yours?

After you create your Pet Peeves list, **convert each Peeve into a Greatness Element**. If the Pet Peeve is what *not* to do, what should be done instead? You don't just want a grumpy list of peeves; you want to become better because of it.

What a strong start! You've just created a custom list of do's and don'ts- your own *radically simple ideas* for becoming an exceptional trainer.

Of course, if it were that simple, this book wouldn't exist. None of us would have been able to think of pet peeves if every training was already amazing. Designing and facilitating exceptional learning for others takes significant **time, intentionality**, and **practice**.

Let's move from ideas on paper to executing them at a high level. This starts with what you *believe*.

Part 2

Essential Trainer Beliefs

Activities alone will not create exceptional training.

What you *believe* will permeate everything you do.

BELIEF 1

Speaking and facilitating learning is a privilege.
I won't take it lightly.

When you believe speaking and facilitating learning is a privilege, you bring your best. You read books like this one. You plan intentionally. You seek input and feedback.

People are giving you some of their most precious and finite resource- their *time*. Squandering the opportunity is unfathomable.

Of course that doesn't mean you'll do it perfectly, but when you say yes to the opportunity, you must invest great effort to do it well.

It's not a privilege for others to bask in your brilliance; it's a privilege for you to help them grow into theirs.

BELIEF 2

It's not about me.

The goal is to help others grow. It's about them.

If you believe it's not about *you*, then you:

- **ask more questions** – be sincerely curious, provoke reflection, and empower discussion

- **listen to understand** – so you can meet *learners'* needs and honor *their* experiences

- **talk about yourself less** – you're helping the learners own the content; no need to pontificate or peacock

- **have humble confidence** – speak from experience and expertise without needing others to think you're the smartest person in the room; it's okay if you don't have all the answers

3 Types of Trainers

There are three types of trainers: The Competent, The Confident, and The Connected.

Being **competent** as a brilliant subject-matter-expert doesn't guarantee you can translate your knowledge into *learning* for others. All-Star sports *players* don't always make the best coaches.

Being **confident** and charismatic as a public speaker doesn't guarantee you have experiences, expertise, and insight worth sharing. A-List movie stars aren't necessarily the best trainers or motivational speakers.

Some trainers are only confident or only competent. In isolation, neither is a good thing.

Connected trainers are both competent *and* confident. This is the sweet spot. They connect the complexity of their competence to simple, actionable steps for the audience. They connect with their audience because their confidence is grounded and humble.

> **MOTIVE CHECK** Before you pursue being a trainer or speaker, check your motive. *What's behind your desire to train and speak?*
>
> It's okay if your motivation is that you enjoy it [confidence] or that you have knowledge you want to share [competence], but notice that alone, those are both about *you*, which is not enough to be exceptional. Make sure your motive is *for the learners*.

BELIEF 3
People are smart.
They bring all kinds of experiences and expertise; they just don't know *this*... yet.

In adult learning theory, one of the tenets is that adult learners **want their experiences and expertise to be acknowledged and valued**. Be sure to give them opportunities to reflect and share, not just receive information.

Believing people are smart doesn't mean they are always right or have the full picture. Since you have taken on the responsibility of teaching, part of your role is to simultaneously believe people are smart *and* address misconceptions and knowledge gaps.

PRO TIPS

- **Sincerely compliment them** for being present, willing to learn and grow.

- **Avoid acronyms and jargon.** Even if you *think* everyone knows them, don't risk alienating someone who doesn't. If you're talking to a room of NBA coaches, you obviously don't need to use the words "National Basketball Association," but if there's an acronym many coaches use that may be new to a rookie coach, spell it out.

- **Ask great questions**. Prompt reflection, sharing, and helping them own the learning.

- **Do not condescend.** Everyone wants to feel smart and valued; no one likes feeling dumb. Even if you're the smartest person in the room on this topic, help them feel like they could be too. To reinforce this mindset, a colleague of mine tells trainers, "Be the hope" for the learners… that they can do what you're teaching them.

- **Know your stuff**, so you're prepared to answer questions and use evidence to back-up your claims.

BELIEF 4

Communicating clear expectations is my responsibility.

If I expect it, I must explain it- *the what and the why.*

Avoid The SHOULD HAVE KNOWN Trap

People are smart, but **no one in the room is a mind-reader.** Avoid the trap of assuming they are, especially about what you think is 'common sense.'

Watch out for the accusatory thought: "They should have known…" and "This should be common sense." Even if that's true, blaming someone neither equips them with the skill nor alleviates the frustration you feel at the unmet expectation.

Articulating expectations in a clear and compelling way is your responsibility. The highest-level trainers and leaders own this.

Lead proactively. Be clear, direct, and explicit while having an upbeat, positive tone. Describe both the **what** and **why** for each of your expectations.

Examples:

- "We're taking an hour break for lunch. *That means* ... 60 minutes from now, we're all back in our seats and ready to rock, *not* pulling into the parking lot. If you go to a sit-down restaurant, ask for your check when you order." [Why this matters] "If we're all back in an hour, we honor each other's time and focus. We're not stuck awkwardly waiting for the stragglers or catching them up on what they missed. Go have an amazing lunch. See you at 12:44."

- "I'm going to bring you back from your deep discussions by doing __. Here's what it will look like..." (See Part 10: *Call Backs & Attention Signals* for examples.)

- "As you chat at your tables, go around with rapid-fire answers first, *so that* everyone's voice is heard. Then, if you have time, dig in with curiosity questions like, 'Tell me more about that.'"

- "After we go over logistics for this virtual workshop, I'm going to ask everyone to turn their camera on. If you're having a bad hair day and need to grab a hat, go for it. Having your camera on means we can lean in, see others' reactions, and get closer to the connections we have when we're together in-person."
... "Okay, it's been about 5 minutes and we know all the logistics for how we're going to make this virtual training amazing. If you're willing, please turn on your camera."

BELIEF 5
My success depends on whether they learn it.
If they don't learn, then I wasn't *teaching*.

This mindset can be tough for some people. It can be tempting to think "I just want to *teach* them. Whether they *learn* it is up to them."

> "It is the job of educators to cause their students to learn. Otherwise, we're not teaching, we're just talking to ourselves".
>
> **Bruce Wilkinson**, *The Seven Laws of the Learner*

Some things will always be out of your control, like what happened in the participants' morning prior to arriving at the event, or their willingness to learn the topic. Exceptional trainers don't use this as an excuse. The best learning facilitators take ownership; they design the experience to mitigate and overcome barriers to the learning. They plan creatively, read the room, make adjustments, and seek feedback to ensure the learners have "got it."

They reflect on:

- "Did I give them enough to help them grow?"
- "Did I present it in a way that's memorable and going to stick?"
- "If they didn't learn it, what can I do differently?"
- "How can I be better next time?"

To help them learn it, you need to know what "it" is. On to Belief #6.

BELIEF 6

Planning is essential.
The more prepared I am, the more effective I can be.

> "If I am to speak ten minutes,
> I need a week for preparation;
> if fifteen minutes, three days;
> if half an hour, two days;
> if an hour, I am ready now".
>
> Woodrow Wilson, 28th President of the United States

Woodrow Wilson's point: compelling, clear, and concise communication requires intentional preparation.

Common Rookie Mistakes:

- Rookies start by planning *activities*.

- Rookies plan *too much* content without discerning what's most relevant.

- Rookies assume they can *wing it* because they have confidence and expertise.

To help you avoid rookie mistakes like these, you will find many effective planning structures in the training arena.

At a minimum, answer these questions:

1. What's **the *most* important thing** for them to KNOW? … and DO moving forward?
2. **Why does it *matter* if they learn it?**
3. **Describe Success: "This will be successful *if*…"**
4. *How will I make it* **memorable***?*

See Part 3: *Plan Like A Pro* for more planning insights and structures.

BELIEF 7
Less is more.
...In your content, your slides, and your speaking.

There's Power in the Pause

When you're excited or nervous, talking fast is common, which is unfortunate because then everyone can tell you're nervous *and* they have a harder time tracking with you. So take a *deep* breath before you begin.

3 Areas to Harness the Power in the Pause:

1. **after your sentences, for confident pacing**
   A space comes after a period at the end of each sentence; a *breath* should too.

2. **after your questions, giving time to *think***
   You want *thoughtful* answers, not just quick ones.

3. **after you punch a main point, so it can land and sink in**
   Great comedians excel at this. They know the pause after the punchline is what lets the joke land; if you skip it, you may as well skip the joke.

Zip It

When you direct participants to write or reflect, don't release them to do the task, then start talking again as they work. Rookie trainers do this because they forgot part of the directions they wanted to give or because they got bored when they weren't talking. Release them to a task, then *zip it*… embrace the silence. Let your learners focus on the task *you* gave them.

Edit

If you're an exceptional trainer, the mantras in your mind are: "Just because I love it, doesn't mean it makes the cut," and "I don't need to say it all."

Brainstorm everything you want to include, then edit like you're a minimalist cleaning a hoarder's house. If it doesn't memorably serve your *main point*, **toss it**.

This applies not only to your content but to your speaking and explanations. Shakespeare wrote, "Brevity is the soul of wit." Be witty and concise; never use five sentences when one is enough.

Editing also applies to company events like leadership cohorts and onboarding. It can feel like a great feat to gather people for training. Since they're away from their important regular role and possibly had to travel, you might feel obligated to cram in as much content as possible. *Don't do it!* You want rich experiences, deep discussions, and actionable changes; you do not want a ho-hum passive parade of presentations and information overload.

Think back to the last one-hour talk you attended. How much do you remember... actually *remember?* Even better- what are you still *implementing* from the training? My guess is at most two things. As the speaker, find your 1-3 key points. and go all-in to make them memorable. People won't remember more than that anyway.

Slide Design

- Use large font and minimal words. Microsoft called it "Power Point," not Power Paragraph, Power Bullet List, or Power Photo Collage.

- Use only a few consistent font styles and colors.

- Use clear, bold visuals and images; people remember them more than text.

- Incorporate blank black slides; you don't always need something on screen.

- Consider: *Do you need a slide deck at all?*

Be The Best DJ

Back in 2008, my wedding DJ taught me the DJ mindset: '**Keep them dancing** with amazing music and seamless transitions. **The less I talk, the more they dance.**'

As the learning facilitator, specifically in a workshop, this means *the less you talk*, the more the learners can experience and own the learning.

The less I talk, the more the learners can experience and *own* the learning.

BELIEF 8

Authenticity and energy matter.

Be YOU, and create the vibe you want for the learning.

Look back at your list of Pet Peeves and Greatness Elements. Did you have anything about low or excessive energy, monotone delivery, a drab ambiance in the room, or an overly scripted, disingenuous speaker?

The trainer and the atmosphere both matter.

Atmosphere

Have music playing as people enter. The music you choose, from peaceful to funky, sets the tone for the experience. Pay attention to the music in the next few stores you enter. I guarantee the one without any music playing will feel awkward and drab.

> "If people find you likable, if people feel noticed, heard, or more importantly, feel a connection to you, they are significantly more inclined to learn from you".
>
> **psychologist and author, Dr. Jody Carrington**

If you're able, greet people as they enter and use their names as you engage with them. Not every trainer is in the headspace to do this right before they speak or facilitate, but if you can, it helps people feel seen and valued.

Authenticity

> "Be yourself because everyone else is already taken".
>
> **poet and playwright, Oscar Wilde**

Authenticity is about having your own energy and style, not someone else's. As you watch other speakers, seek inspiration not imitation. The world doesn't need another *them*; the world needs YOU.

Level Up

If you are a naturally high energy person, be aware that energy can be dynamic and engaging; it can also seem off-putting or disingenuous. If your style is more naturally stoic and steady, be aware that your vibe can be comforting and instill confidence; it can also be disengaging or boring.

When I teach, I am naturally high-energy and joyful. One of my 8th grade students once compared me to Flo from the Progressive commercials, and a recent workshop participant said I was like Joy from *Inside Out*. Yet, when I'm nervous or excited, this strength can become a detriment- my pitch and pace increase, making me seem insincere or less competent. Know yourself well so you can refine your style for maximum impact.

Try asking a friend to attend one of your workshops or speeches. Tell them you're going to show up with your natural style, and that you'd like them to watch for tiny tweaks, specifically:

- As you spoke, at what moment(s) did you light up in a way that people connected with?

- What needs to be toned down or amped up?

Every superhero has a different power. When they first discover it, they have to learn how to use it. Do the same.

BONUS CHECK
Questions to Find Your Unique Voice and Content

- Your passion is contagious.
- Your experiences are unique.
- Your expertise is worth sharing.

Gain insight. Ask yourself:

- What's **unique from my story** that might inspire or help someone else?
- What **problem can I help people solve** using my experience and expertise? I know people struggle with _____, and I can help them with that.
- What do I light up about and could **talk about for hours**? Where does that come from? Why am I passionate about that?
- What do **people ask me about** often?

Ask a few close friends:

- What do you see in me (strengths; uniqueness)?
- What do you come to me for?

Essential Facilitator Beliefs
RECAP

What you **BELIEVE** *bears fruit* … in your words, your tone, your choices, and your actions.

As an exceptional trainer, continually anchor yourself in these beliefs:

1. I believe: Speaking and facilitating learning is a privilege.
2. I believe: It's not about me; it's about the learner.
3. I believe: People are smart.
4. I believe: Communicating clear expectations is my responsibility.
5. I believe: My success depends on whether they *learn* it.
6. I believe: Planning is essential.
7. I believe: Less is more.
8. I believe: Authenticity and energy matter.

Part 3

Plan Like A Pro

There are many effective planning structures in the training arena. My approach flows like this:

Phase 1	Brain Storm
Phase 2	Anchor Questions
Phase 3	Outline
Phase 4	Empathy-Centered Design

Planning Phase 1: Brain Storm

In school, when you were learning the writing process, brainstorming came first. It was messy and unrestricted. Then followed an outline, a draft, feedback, and revisions. Apply this process to planning your speech or workshop.

Brainstorm first. Think of *everything* you want to share. Think of all the ways you might accomplish it. Get it all out in whatever format works for you. No need to *evaluate* ideas here. Let the 'storm' be wild.

Once you have your brainstorm, be prepared to do what writing and speech coaches call "kill your darlings," meaning you'll have to let go of some ideas you love. When you're communicating and teaching at the highest level, be incredibly selective about what makes the cut.

> **Albert Einstein** *is credited with saying,*
> "If you don't understand it fully,
> you can't explain it simply".

> **Comedian Jerry Seinfeld** *said:*
> "The most important word in art
> is proportion".

Simplicity requires humility and restraint. Great trainers can take their deep well of knowledge and their storm of creative ideas, and strategically *let things go*, in order to maximize learning.

> **PRO TIP** Set a deadline after which you won't add more research or new ideas to your content. This will help you effectively move from ideation to execution. It will save you from continuously reworking things that you'd previously considered complete.

Planning Phase 2: Anchor Questions

> "Begin with the end in mind".
> St. Francis of Assisi (and later, Stephen R. Covey)

Now that you've gotten all your ideas out in a brainstorm, take a deep breath and zoom out. Complete this statement to anchor your content development and delivery:

This will be *successful if* . . .

This is THE most important and beneficial question to ask as you plan. Your answer will guide *everything*.

In the examples below, notice how each Success Anchor would yield a slightly different speech or workshop.

Example 1:

You're giving a speech on "the power of shared-goals for leadership teams," and you're torn between these two Success Anchors:

A. *This will be successful if...* they hear compelling examples that convince them to pursue this with their own executive team.

B. *This will be successful if...* they learn the specifics and nuances of my five-step model for creating shared goals.

Both Speech A and Speech B will likely include stories and your five-step model. But where you spend the majority of your time, and what you decide to consolidate or cut will change depending on whether you choose A or B.

Example 2:

You've been asked to lead a "Google Docs 101" training for a company that recently switched from their previous file platform to Google. Possible Success Anchors might be:

A. *This session will be successful if...* they can easily navigate Google Docs for basic use and are comfortable finding more advanced features on their own.

B. *This session will be successful if...* they learn at least ten tips and tricks that convert their resistance into enthusiasm for Google Docs.

C. *This session will be successful if...*they migrate and convert their main files from the previous platform into Google Docs.

Sure, if you have tons of time, you'd teach all three, but what if you only have one hour? Deciding which one is the Success Anchor will drive how you design the training and where you spend the most time.

PRO TIP Be sure to ask your client or the training-project manager what *their* Success Anchor is for your speech or workshop. It might sound like this:

> "I want to make sure we're on the same page so I meet your needs. Think about your dream outcome for this speech/workshop/event. How would you complete the phrase: *This will be successful if…?*"

It's such a simple question and such a powerful way to ensure you hit the mark and can exceed their expectations.

PRO TIP Various industries label the "*This will be successful if…*" Success Anchor concept with phrases like: learning targets, instructional outcomes, success criteria, or academic standards. They include formal structures, such as using strong verbs and focusing on the learner, not the trainer. These are great tips! If you write formal learning objectives, ditch words like "*understand,*" "*learn,*" or "*hear.*" Those are vague and passive. Aim for strong verbs that align with high-level thinking and engagement, like "analyze," "explore," "discuss," or "create."

The more formal structures are absolutely useful. I find the conversational nature of "*This will be successful if…*" helps me and those I coach articulate the *heartfelt* goal for the learning without overthinking it. When I need to submit formal learning objectives, I refine those after I'm clear and passionate about my Success Anchor statement.

Additional Anchor Questions

In addition to the Success Anchor, pause to articulate your answers to these questions:

Value

- Why is it important they learn this topic?

- What's the cost if they don't learn this?

Consider both individual and broader community impact:

Context

Watch for what might hinder learning, so you can strategically plan to overcome it.

- Who will attend? Who is this for? (**audience**)

- What's the **context** for this learning/event? e.g. Is attendance voluntary or mandated? Am I the last speaker in a multi-day event? Did the company have a recent leadership change that's caused skepticism?

- What are some common **questions** (curiosities, confusion, or pushback) related to this topic?

- What are some common **misconceptions** to address and debunk?

Logistics

- How is the room set up? Is it conducive for the experience I'm designing? e.g. Are they seated in tight rows or round tables. Is there space to move around? Will people have difficulty hearing each other during group discussions?

- What is the audio-visual set-up? e.g. What type of mic will I have? Can I move around or am I tied to a podium? Can every seat see a screen? Can every seat see what I'm doing on stage? If I play a video clip, will the audio work?

Main Point

- What do I want them to *know*? (1-3 things; your "power" points.)

- What do I want them to *do* moving forward?

- If they remember nothing else, what's **the ONE thing** I want them to remember?

- What's my **throughline**- the consistent theme, metaphor, mantra, or thread woven throughout?

- What content and activities do I need to *let go of* (eliminate)?

Planning Phase 3: Outline

With your Success Anchor in mind, begin wrangling your wild brainstorm.

Identify the big pieces:

- What will the participants **do**?
- What will they **reflect on** and **discuss**?
- What will they **see** and **hear?**
- What might they **receive** (a physical takeaway, trinket, or digital resource) to help them remember?
- How *else* can I make this memorable? (See Part 6: *Make It Memorable*)

Create your outline.

Consider how you will:

- **START Strong** - *to hook them from the first moment*
- **ENGAGE Continuously** - *incorporating meaningful activities, discussions, and movement*
- **TRANSITION Seamlessly** - *to ensure flow and connection between sections and activities*
- **END Strong** - *to secure a lasting impact*

Analyze your flow.

- Put the duration/minutes next to each major section.
- Note each time learners are actively engaging in something, versus just listening.
- Note how often they sit versus stand/move. (I use up and down arrows on my outline.)

> **WATCH A PRO** To watch an expert at quick pace and utilizing frequent transitions, find a video online (TEDx or a recorded seminar) of hall-of-fame speaker Amanda Gore. Imagine what her annotated outline would look like.

Planning Phase 4: Empathy-Centered Design

Exceptional trainers proactively embody empathy; they intentionally mitigate barriers to the learning. To meet learners' diverse needs, here are things I consider:

Age; Generation; Culture

- Learn what you can about the group and their values and customs.

Introverts/Extroverts; Internal/External Processors

- Give think-time for silent reflection and writing before group chats (for internal processors).

- Include opportunities for discussion and energizing connection (for extroverts).

- Use the phrase "Play or Pass" to honor autonomy for those who aren't yet ready to share.

Accessibility - *such as auditory and visual challenges*

- Use closed captions on all videos.
- Use large font and minimal words.

  > **PRO TIP** If someone with a vision disability couldn't read your slide, then you have too much info and the font is too small. Remember: These are not slides people are reading independently like a book or report. Your slides are *visual aides* to your message and content flow.

- Use high-contrast colors on slides and handouts.

  > **PRO TIP** A black background with white font is easier on the eyes than a white background with black font.

- Consider whether the acoustics work for group discussions in packed, loud rooms.

Varied Levels Of Expertise

- Ask questions to acknowledge and draw from expertise in the room.
- For tech-centric activities, have a low-tech or no-tech option available.

Final Empathy Reflection

Remember to put yourself in the learners shoes. Step back from designing the experience and ask yourself-

- Would I like the experience of this workshop or speech?
- Would someone who's dramatically different from me like it?

How you plan can vary by personality and style. As mentioned, there are many planning structures in the training arena. If my flow doesn't fit your style, here are a few frameworks worth honorable mention.

Bonus: Other Popular Planning Frameworks

- **What? So what? Now what? What if…?**
    - *What:* …you want them to know/do/believe/feel
    - *So What:* …why it matters
    - *Now What:* …specific call to action
    - *What If:* …paint the picture of the positive impact if implemented

This framework is also powerful as a post-learning, end-of-workshop reflection tool. (See Part 5: *End Strong.*)

- **Know | Do | Believe | Feel**

  A popular framework for event planning used by a mega-church in the United States. When planning, ask: What do I/we want them to:

    - Know? (specific knowledge/concepts)
    - Do? (during the experience and after)
    - Believe? (mindset shifts; convictions)
    - Feel? (vibe of the event; emotions of the participants, etc.)

- *The 4 Ms:* **M**eaningful, **M**emorable, **M**otivational, **M**easurable

  The CCAF Design Mode (Context, Challenge, Activity, and Feedback) for interactive e-learning instructional design from Dr. Michael Allen is grounded in creating learning that is Meaningful, Memorable, Motivational, and Measurable. Plan how you're going to do each of the 4 Ms and you're off to a powerful start!

- **S.I.M.P.L.E.** framework - created by my colleague Deanna Boston
    - **S**uccinct: Edit your content.
    - **I**mpactful: Why does it matter? What should they do with the insight?
    - **M**eaningful: Share a memorable story.
    - **P**eople: It's about what they need to hear, not what I have to say.
    - **L**earning: What is one takeaway they can leave with to make the learning last?
    - **E**ngaging: Include participants in the learning.

An activity is not a *strategy* unless it has a clear purpose.

The next chapters are packed with reusable *strategies*.

Part 4
Start Strong

Whether it's a job interview, a first day, a website, the opening pages in a book, or a training session, first impressions are an opportunity for connection, curiosity, and buy-in. Don't squander it with a long-winded, dull opener. Try one of these strategies to maximize the impact of your opening moment.

Strategies to Start Strong in a Workshop

1. **Future-Focused Reflection Prompt**

    - Example: They complete a Success Anchor sentence- "For me, this workshop will be a success if... "

    - You can facilitate this as independent writing, drawing, or socially sharing with someone nearby.

    - *Bonus:* They can revisit and rate it at the end to evaluate success.

2. **Pick Your Quote / Stand By Your Quote**
   - Curate a list of quotes related to the learning topic.
   - Provide the list of quotes on paper, or post them separately in various places around the room.
   - Participants select or stand by their favorite quote, and share why they chose it.

3. **Symbolic & Creative Thinking**
   - Have learners *create* an analogy from scratch, explain one you provide, *develop* it based on a photo, or a combination.
   - **Examples:**

     They *create* it-
     - "Meetings are like…"
     - "Learning a new tech platform is like…"

     They *explain* it-
     - "Working in customer service is like gardening *because…*"

     They *expand* and *explain* it-
     - "If our team were a meal, we would be _____ because _____."
     - "If there were a beverage for our profession, it would be called _____ because _____."

     They *select a photo* and *explain* it-

- The facilitator scatters a set of random photos (images). Each participant choose one as their base for a visual metaphor.
  - **Person 1:** "This *prickly cactus* is like our current onboarding practices because…"
  - **Person 2:** "This *lightning storm* is like our current onboarding practices because…"
  - **Person 3:** "This *refrigerator* is like our current onboarding practices because…"
- See **Image Metaphor Cards** at PositiveStrategery.com.

4. **Word Unscrambles**
   - Select a few keywords related to your topic.
   - Scramble the letters, and put the word-scrambles on screen or at each table.
   - Have everyone try to unscramble the letters and identify the key words.
   - Once the words are unscrambled (show the correct ones on screen), elaborate on their meaning to open the training.
   - *Strategic Timing:* Word Scrambles can be on screen as a brain-activator for those who arrive early, as the opening activity to launch your session, or as mid-session to transition to a new topic.

   > PRO TIP Tell people to raise their hand if they solve them, but not shout it out right away. This gives everyone time to try it.

5. **Consensograms, Dot Voting, & String Maps**
   - These are survey techniques with visual results.
   - Each person receives dot stickers or a marker to add their rating or response on the poster(s).

   > **PRO TIP** Using posters instead of a digital tool gets people up and moving, and keeps the results visible throughout the training.

   - Example Poster Prompts:
     - **Who's In The Room**
       - number of years in this industry (you prep the poster with ranges: e.g. 0-1, 2-5, 6-10, etc.)
       - role (you prep the poster with job titles)
     - **Topic Voting & Trends**
       - greatest challenge area (you prep the poster with the top categories)
       - comfort level with _____ (you prep the poster with topic and scale)
       - topics for the day (they pick their one top priority, or use a scale to rate their interest for *each* topic)
   - **Advanced Version: String Maps**
     - *great for conferences and big events*

- On a giant board, the top lists items in a group, such as roles, departments, industries, or tenure in years. The bottom has words related to a prompt, such as:
    - common pain points (meetings, collaboration, funding)
    - the topic of the day that they are most eager to dive into
    - preferred social media platform
- People connect a string from the top to the bottom, connecting the category and answer that applies to them.
- The board shows the trends disaggregated by *group* (top category).

6. **Eight Brains to One:** *Group Definition Activity*

- Step 1: Provide a Prompt (e.g. *Great sales people have these traits:* _____)

- Step 2 Everyone has 30 seconds to independently brainstorm single-word answers.

- Step 3: They find a partner and identify *words they have in common*. Those are the only words they keep and take forward into Step 4.

- Step 4: Join another pair, meet each other, and find the words both pairs have in common, using their list from Step 3 (not each *individual* list).

- Step 5: New group of 4 finds another group of 4 and identifies the words they have in common.

- Wrap: The group of 8 now has a consensus definition or their shared answer to the prompt. The list is their eight brains as one.

- *Facilitator Note:* Encourage curiosity and discussion. The goal isn't to get their combined list the fastest; they also want to learn from each other.

7. **Curiosity Spark**

    - People learn better and remember more when they are sincerely curious about something.

    - Have something on-screen that sparks curiosity- an intriguing photo or video clip, a quote or paragraph, a real-world dilemma, or a statistic.

    - Prompt participants to write down what they're curious about: *Why... How... I wonder...*

8. **An Empowering Question**
   - Simple questions can be powerful starts. Rather than *telling* participants why the workshop topic is important, a simple question can provoke reflection and tap into learners' experiences. Open with a thought-provoking question, then give them a couple minutes to write or chat about it.
   - Examples:
     - "What is service?" (for a customer service or hospitality workshop)
     - "What nuances factor into whether communication is effective?" (for a communications workshop)
     - "Who is your leadership role model, and why?" (for a leadership workshop)
   - Alternative Format: I sometimes frame the questions as a **sentence starter**. The learners brainstorm words to *finish the statement.* Example: "Leadership is _____."

Specifically useful for stressful or emotionally–charged contexts:

9. **Deep Breathing (facilitated)**
   - Example: Box Breathing
     - Deep breath in for 4 seconds, hold for 4 seconds, exhale for 4 seconds, hold for 4 seconds

- Called "box" breathing because you can trace a box in the air with your hand, each side representing a 4-second step.

10. **Free Write - What's On Your Mind**

    - Give participants paper, instrumental music, and time to write. Tell them to "just write… try to keep your pen moving… don't overthink it." They can write about *anything*. It's just for them; they won't be asked to share.

    - Some will get creative, some will process their previous meeting. You're simply giving space for them to unload their mind so there's space for new learning.

    - *Alternative Versions:*

      Pack Your Worries
      - Participants draw a backpack and quick-write, filling it with their stressors and worries. The worries can be unrelated to the workshop topic.

      Gratitudes & Wins
      - Participants write as many specific gratitudes and wins as they can during the free-write time. Great for finding the positive even amidst a hard day or season. You can decide whether these are related to the learning topic, specific to work, or wide-open.

11. **Two Sticky Notes**
    - related to the workshop topic
    - *Note #1* = a hope or positive; *Note #2* = a concern or question
    - Participants reflect, write, and then post in a designated location in the room.
    - The facilitator reviews (during a break or while learners are engaged in an activity later on); they intentionally address any unanswered questions at the end.

PRO TIPS

1. **In workshops, have something *meaningful* for participants to do as soon as they *arrive*.** If you then need to delay the start by a few minutes for stragglers, you're still maximizing the minutes for everyone else.

2. **Be wary of cheesy icebreakers and overly-vulnerable opening discussion questions.**
   As a facilitator, keep in mind that connection and content can co-exist. Starting with connection is useful in meetings and putting people before tasks. It's useful in school classrooms to develop a safe learning community among students. In workshops, however, the mantra "connections before content" is often misused, resulting in silly icebreaker games and eye-rolls. As you facilitate for adults, provide opportunities for them to connect in *meaningful* ways within the context of what they'll be learning.

3. **Don't start with your resume.** Instead, gain credibility with how you speak and facilitate. If you're being introduced, provide a succinct 30-second bio with a few memorable highlights from your career, not a detailed history. You can drop comments about job titles and experiences within the anecdotes you tell. Spending 5-7 minutes on your resume is all about *you*, and... this might be painful to hear- most people don't care.

Strategies to Start Strong in a Speech

Author and speaker Jon Acuff calls your opening sentence your "lean in" line. It's an opportunity to captivate the audience, to get them to *lean in*. Never start with the overly direct and dull statement: *"Today I'm going to talk about...."* You're an exceptional speaker; you can do so much better than that.

Whatever opening line you use, remember to be authentically YOU. Find an opening that *hooks* the audience and that you genuinely like, so your delivery is effortless not forced. Say your opening line, then embrace the power in the pause. Let it land, so they lean in.

Examples of Strong Opening Phrases:

- "I have 15 minutes to *convince* you that…" [challenge]
- "I'm going to make a *confession*…" [intrigue or empathy]
- "Your philosophy and experiences will be your own. I'm hoping mine may help shape and refine yours." [autonomy]
- "I've got a *question* for you…" [curiosity and engagement]
- "How many of you have ever _____? …Yup, we *all* have!" [nostalgia and connection] (This one is similar to the psychology of the sales strategy: *Feel, Felt, Found.*)
- "Y"all know that song _____? …
    - "These lyrics are going to be our mantra."
    - "Let me tell you why that's my theme song."

  [musical connection]

- "Hey y'all! Are you loving this phenomenal event as much as I am?" [genuine positivity]
- "How great was _____?" - compliment the speaker before you, the lunch, etc. [event affirmation]
- "You all are so inspiring. You are _____ and _____." - use specific adjectives [audience affirmation]

- "Can we all pause for a moment and remember-
    - that *feeling* when _____?"
    - that *time/event* when _____?"

  [nostalgic connection]

- Share a staggering statistic or quote, followed by, "This should *concern* us because…" or "This is wildly important because…" [urgency; emotion; problem-awareness]

- "I can't live up to that intro, so it's all downhill from here." - a light-hearted self-deprecating joke with a smile [humor and confidence]

- "I've been studying/doing _____ for decades and I've concluded that _____ (state something obvious). *But*… (pick one-)
    - it's not that simple."
    - our intuition about this often fails us."
    - there are a few significant misconceptions we commonly hold."

  [intrigue; invitation to gain expert insight]

- "I have this great fear…" or "I have this great dream…" [fear inspiration as a motivator]

- Create a metaphor between your topic and something simple, visual, or well known.
  - "I've been thinking about _____ Our topic today is a lot like that."
  - "Have you ever noticed how _____ is like _____?"

  [metaphors and symbolic thinking]

- Dive right into a captivating, concise story that ties to a metaphor or point. [story as a memorable metaphor]

- "When I say _____ (topic), what are you curious about? ... Go ahead and think for a moment. Think phrases like- *I wonder. Why? How? What if? Who? Why not?* (pause) In our time together, I hope to answer some of your questions."

The list in this chapter was created from observing high-level speakers at many leadership conferences; it's not an exhaustive list. If none of the examples suit you, find other speakers (hello YouTube!) and watch just the first and last 3 minutes of their talks. Write down how they open and close. If you don't get distracted by cat videos, you can gain inspiration from ten speakers in just one hour. That's a lot of insight!

Start Strong Strategies
RECAP

Strategies:

1. Future-Focused Reflection Prompt
2. Pick Your Quote / Stand By Your Quote
3. Symbolic & Creative Thinking
4. Word Unscrambles
5. Consensograms, Dot Voting, & String Maps
6. Eight Brains to One: Group Definition Activity
7. Curiosity Spark
8. An Empowering Question
9. Deep Breathing (facilitated)
10. Free Write - What's On Your Mind
11. Two Sticky Notes

Part 5

End Strong

Can you imagine if an author wrote a captivating, epic story, then the last chapter abruptly read: *"Then it ended. Thanks for reading."*?

No way! They'd wrap up loose ends and provide a feeling of closure because they know: *the end matters*.

You put great effort into creating captivating training. Don't close with a lazy ending like, "Anyone have any questions?" or "We're out of time; thanks for coming." The end matters; close intentionally.

Strategies to End Strong in a Workshop

1. **What, So What, Now What**
    - Have participants answer each one:
        - ***What*** - did you learn?
        - ***So What*** - why does it matter?
        - ***Now What*** - will you do? (action steps)

2. **"I used to think _____. Now I think _____."**

    - This is a Visible Thinking Routine from Harvard's Project Zero. It's a reusable sentence frame that guides people to reflect on a perspective change or new insight.

        > **BONUS** This is also a great tool when facilitating project reviews or growth reflections for teams.

3. **One Thing**

    - Participants write, post, and/or share their unforgettable takeaway from the workshop.

    - Provide them with a prompt to guide them.

        Examples:

        - "One thing I commit to is __."

        - "The tagline for this speech or workshop is __."

        - Group Anthem: Choose and complete one of these three:
            - "I am…"
            - "I believe…"
            - "I will…"

    - *Fun Twist:* **Selfie Speech Bubbles**
    Give each person a large speech bubble (available to purchase online). Everyone writes their ONE Thing, then takes a picture holding up their speech bubble as if they're saying it.

4. **Three-Two-One (3-2-1)**
   - You define a category for each, then have them reflect and write answers to solidify the learning.
   - Examples:
     - 3 people who embody this concept, 2 things worth remembering, 1 wondering you're going to investigate further
     - 3 highlights, 2 commitments, 1 metaphor

5. **Reminder to Future Self**
   - Help them keep the learning alive long-term, recalling what they've learned but forgotten.
   - Direct participants to put a reminder in their phone or schedule a future email to themselves; the content is what they want to remember from the learning experience.

6. **The 3 As: Ah-Ha, Appreciation, Ask**
   - Participants choose one of the three As to share:

Choose and share ONE of the 3 As:

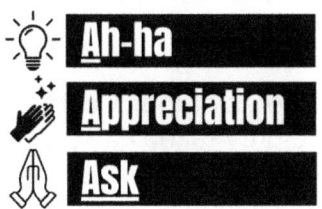

> Ah-ha - a lightbulb of new insight

> Appreciation - of someone in the room, a work process, etc.

> Ask - a request they're making of their team members or fellow participants

7. **Share the Learning Love**

    - The best way to learn is to teach. Ask participants to text someone in their life, sharing one cool thing they learned.

    - *3 Benefits:* reinforcing the learning by typing it, spurring someone else's growth (now they learn what you've learned), and potentially sparking a great conversation.

8. **The Phone Call**

    - At the beginning of the workshop, ask learners to think of someone who *exemplifies* one of the key topics for the day (leadership, collaboration, safety, communication, etc.).

    - At the end of the workshop, ask for a volunteer willing to call that colleague on speaker-phone, so the whole room can hear. The participant tells that person: "I'm in a workshop about _____. You are on speaker phone. I'm calling to tell you that to me, you exemplify this topic because _____."

    - *Benefits*: peer affirmations *and* connecting the learning with life-experience.

9. **Give 1, Get 1: The Great Idea Swap**

    - Everyone gets three sticky notes or index cards. They write a different idea or key takeaway on each card. These can be their favorite things from the learning session and/or additional ideas they have from their experience.

- Standing, people pair up.

- Partner A reads their three cards, and Partner B steals whichever one they like most.

- They put a tally-mark on the stolen card. (This step is important, so model and emphasize it.)

- To reciprocate, Partner B reads their three cards, and Partner A steals one, adding a tally-mark to it.

- After a quick yet interesting exchange of ideas, they each go find another partner and repeat the exchange process (again and again).

- When many notecards have been exchanged, the facilitator calls time, and everyone sits down.

- *Facilitate the Debrief:*

    - Ask if anyone has a card stolen at least ____ times (you pick the number). They read those popular cards aloud for the group.

    - Ask if anyone has a card that wasn't stolen much but the card-holder thinks it's so great it *must* be shared with everyone.

10. **Symbolic & Creative Thinking**

    - See the directions and examples in Part 4: *Start Strong*.

    - As an *End Strong* strategy, have their metaphor creation connects to their key takeaway from the learning that day. They then explain their takeaway to the group using their metaphor.

- **Image Metaphor Cards *For Teams:*** If you're facilitating a workshop for a team, have people consider what they admire about the person sitting to their right. Each participant then selects a photo (from the pile set out by the facilitator) to create a visual metaphor for what they admire about their colleague. Everyone verbalizes their affirmation-photo-metaphor and gives the photo to the colleague it represents.

- *See a ready-to-print-and-cut card deck at PositiveStrategery.com.*

PRO TIP In workshops, have participants complete the evaluation survey *before* you facilitate the closing. This honors their time, increases the quantity and quality of survey completion, and makes your intentional *closing* activity truly the closing activity.

Strategies to End Strong in a Speech

Paint a picture of what's possible.
Call them up and call them to action.
Close the loop on a story you introduced earlier.
Reiterate your most important line.

Examples of Strong Closing Phrases:

- "What if…" / "Imagine if…" [paint the picture of what's possible and the potential positive impact]

- "We all have the power to…"

- Restate your main point or share a compelling quote, then say, "So how do we do that? *By*…"

- "So here's what I want you to do…" (such as-)
    - …write these 5 things down."
    - …set a reminder in your phone."
    - …tell someone on your team XYZ."

- "As I read the four areas we've covered, I'm going to ask you to *stand up* when I read the one you are committed to focusing on."

- "The next time you encounter ____ (challenge/problem related to your topic), my hope is that you ____."

- "My parting question for you is…"

End Strong Strategies
RECAP

Strategies:

1. What, So What, Now What
2. "I used to think _____. Now I think _____."
3. One Thing
4. Three-Two-One (3-2-1)
5. Reminder to Future Self
6. The 3 As: Ask, Appreciation, Ah-ha
7. Share the Learning Love
8. The Phone Call
9. Give 1 Get 1: The Great Idea Swap
10. Symbolic & Creative Thinking

Part 6

Make It Memorable

You want what you're teaching to make a lasting impact... to stick. Fortunately, there are many ways to make things memorable. Using *all* of them would feel overwhelming and chaotic, so start by identifying a few that fit your content and style.

People Remember:

- ☐ well-told stories and anecdotes
- ☐ strong emotions (humor, dissonance, etc.)
- ☐ practical, easy-to-implement ideas
- ☐ repeated mantras & phrases - even better with rhythm, alliteration, or music
- ☐ simple steps or lists they can reuse
- ☐ compelling statistics
- ☐ visuals (far more than text) - icons, images, video clips, demonstrations
- ☐ analogies

Also Noteworthy- People Remember:

- ☐ the highlights and the end of experiences (Peak-End Rule)
- ☐ what they discuss
- ☐ what they do and experience
- ☐ what they teach others
- ☐ what they repeat over time (repeat to remember)

From Part 3: *Plan Like a Pro*, remember to consider:

- What will they **do**?
- What will they **reflect on** and **discuss**?
- What will they **see** and **hear?**
- What might they **receive** (a physical takeaway or trinket) to help them remember?

BONUS   There's a ton of research and science behind how to make learning last. Part 13: *Rad Simple Ways to Keep Improving* has some keywords and gems related to "the science of learning."

The BEST strategy is a THOUGHT-PROVOKING QUESTION.

Part 7

Discussions & Groups

You've likely experienced a group discussion where one person dominates, or where everyone quickly answers the question then awkwardly stares at each other, thinking "What are we supposed to talk about now?" Factors like participant personalities, group dynamics, discussion structures, and prompt quality can impact the effectiveness of a discussion.

Exceptional trainers strategically orchestrate exceptional discussions.

> PRO TIP
>
> 1. **Allow for Varying Levels of Vulnerability**
>
> When it comes to participants' vulnerability in workshops, think of people as pots of water that are at various temperatures. Some are already warm and simmering; they're ready to be vulnerable and share anything.

Others are cool and need time to warm up slowly before they're ready to boil over.

Everyone is not a boiling pot of water at the start. What do you do about that? You give people time to think and process their answers before sharing. You give people the choice to "Play or Pass." You use open-ended questions so they can choose their level of vulnerability. As an example, if you ask "What's a current challenge you're facing?" someone might say "traffic" and someone else might say "feeling inadequate at work." Even with time, not everyone will warm up to boiling during your workshop, and that's okay. Invite great conversations while giving people space to organically warm up to their peak vulnerability level.

PRO TIP

2. Support Internal and External Processors

As you facilitate, keep in mind that internal processors crave time to *think* before they talk. Providing moments of silence where everyone jots down ideas before they chat often enriches discussions.

In my workshops, I often explain openly to participants that-

> "There are *internal processors* in the room who, after hearing a discussion question, want two weeks to ponder it before they're ready to discuss it. (Insert inevitable chuckles from the people who know that's

true of them.) And simultaneously there are *external processors* in the room who prefer to start talking immediately, regardless of whether they have a thoughtful answer because they discover insights through the process of discussion. I'll do my best to create a flow that supports all of you."

Setting the stage with this shared awareness often helps people feel seen and embrace the various needs of the group.

> **PRO TIP**
> 3. **One Prompt At A Time; No Question Stacking**
>   - *Avoid*: "Talk about these three things." **We can't talk about different things at the same time.** And, it's not natural for most people to work through a topic checklist in a conversation. When three questions are asked simultaneously, usually only one will be answered.
>   - *Instead*: Separate each question. Ask them one at a time to focus and pace the discussions.

> **PRO TIP**
> 4. **Provide Provocative Prompts**

One of your most important skills as a trainer is how you ASK QUESTIONS.

Provoke reflection and visualization. Ensure your prompts are open and divergent, allowing for answers to go in many different directions. Create prompts for conversations you'd find interesting and would want to be part of.

I frequently frame discussion prompts around: **Beliefs**, **Behaviors**, **Barriers**, and *How* (radically simple ideas).

Example from a Leadership Workshop:

A. If you're going to lead well-
   What do you have to **believe**?
   What does it look like? (specific **behaviors**)

B. When you're *not* leading well-
   What do you **believe**? (including fears)
   What does that look like? (specific **behaviors**)

C. What gets in the way of leading well? (**barriers**)

D. **How?** What small, specific things can we do to improve? (***radically simple* ideas**)

As the trainer, I have ideas for each component ready, but people rarely need me to give them the answers. If I instead give them time to reflect and discuss, then they own the learning. My greatest value as a facilitator is asking the questions, creating space, and having some implementation tips ready to share.

PRO TIP

5. **Put The Discussion Question On Screen**
   - Large, simple, and easy to read.
   - This anchors the conversation when someone inevitably says, "Wait, what are we supposed to be talking about?" It also requires that you, the trainer, thoughtfully plan your questions ahead of time.

PRO TIP

6. **Give *"Who Talks First"* Guidance**
   - Doing so mitigates initial discussion awkwardness and prevents the most dominant person from always going first.
   - *Sounds like*: "As you chat with your group, the person whose name starts with the earliest letter in the alphabet goes first."
   - *Examples:*
     - tallest person
     - longest hair
     - got up the earliest today
     - stayed up the latest last night
     - traveled farthest to get here
     - been in their current role the longest
     - graduated from the farthest away school
     - *Ask participants for ideas!*

- **Bonus:** You can use these same kinds of prompts to identify who will report out key insights from each group, or who is going to be the group leader and ensure every voice is heard.

> **PRO TIP**
>
> 7. **Be Humble and Generous** Conversations about our experiences can be powerful; when participants are talking, they own the learning. Creating space for discussion is an act of *humility* and *generosity*. It would be more efficient if you just *told* them the information, but instead, you choose to give them time to reflect on experiences and wrestle with ideas. You let them feel it and own it.

Structures for Partner or Group Discussions

Using structures and protocols improves discussions, keeping them focused and inclusive.

1. **Think, Pair, Share**
    - This strategy has three simple phases: give people protected time to think or write independently, then chat in pairs, then share out with the whole group.
    - This is a timeless classic in K-12 education; equally beneficial for adults and easy to implement.

2. **Poster/Station Rotations**
a.k.a. Chat Stations
    - Put large poster paper around the room.

- At each poster the group discusses the topic and writes key ideas on the poster.
- Groups rotate between posters. A timer on screen and the trainer direct when it's time to move.
- **Use 1:**
  - Each poster is prepared with a unique topic or question for the group to discuss. As groups rotate, each poster station sparks a new conversation on a new topic.
- **Use 2:**
  - The facilitator provides a prompt for the whole room, such as "What words describe an amazing team?" or "What are the greatest challenges related to your sales role?"
  - At their poster, each group stands and chats, capturing their key ideas on the poster as they talk.
  - When they rotate, they're *reading* the previous group's poster, not adding new ideas to it. Instead, they mark it with symbols:
    - ? Question Marks - anything they're curious about or want clarified
    - ★ Stars - anything new and insightful that they didn't have on *their* original poster
  - After a couple rotations, groups return to their original poster.

- They clarify any question marks on their poster by sharing quick explanations with the whole room.
- *Benefits:* Movement and interacting with others' ideas.

3. **Lightning Around The Table**
   - In this simple structure, a prompt or sentence-starter is provided, such as "One cool thing my department does is _____." or "One challenge we're facing right now is _____."
   - Everyone finishes the sentence, one at a time, going around the table. The answers are concise. No one is allowed to *respond*, only to finish the sentence when it's their turn.
   - After going around the table 1-3 times, the facilitator calls time. Now people can ask follow-up questions, comment, or share ideas based on what they heard in the no-response round.
   - *Benefits:*
     - All voices are heard.
     - Everyone reflects and shares before any single answer becomes the focus of the conversation.
     - Sometimes common trends and shared-experiences come to light.

4. Table-Top Texting

- *The Gist:* text-message threads on paper

- *Benefit:* Everyone is engaged silently and simultaneously, while covering multiple topics of interest in a short period of time.

- Everyone gets a blank piece of paper and writes an open-ended question at the top- something they're curious to learn from others in the room. (This is like the first text-message in a group-chat.)

- Everyone exchanges papers. They then add a comment in response to the question on that paper. When done, they return it to a pile in the middle of the table and draw another.

- *Repeat, continuously commenting on papers.* It's okay if they don't get to every person's paper. It's also okay if they get the same paper twice, since the text conversation will have evolved with new comments from other people.

- **PRO TIP** If you can anticipate an interesting question or two related to the topic, prepare and add 1-2 extra papers/questions in the mix. This ensures no one is stuck waiting on a paper.

- Wrap Up: The owner of each paper receives their original back and reads their 'text-message' responses. The facilitator asks if anyone has a new insight or a follow-up question to share.

- *Warning:* This activity can be wonderful for engagement, yet it can feel gimmicky to groups who just want to have a live discussion. Use your discernment, and if using this activity, be sure to proactively explain its purpose and benefit.

5. **First Word, Last Word**
    - Learners first read a text, such as a case study, position statement, story, article, or definition.
    - For the discussion, everyone prepares a word, phrase, or sentence that stands out to them from the text. They can choose it for any reason- inspired by it, disagree with it, have a related story to share, etc.
    - The first person shares their word, phrase, or sentence *without giving an explanation for why they chose it*.
    - Going around the table, everyone comments on the first person's word/phrase.
    - The last person to share their thoughts is the one who opened the discussion with the word. After hearing everyone else, they can finally share their thoughts, which may or may not have evolved after hearing everyone else's perspective.

6. **Prompt Cards on Tables**
   - On each table, the trainer provides cards with various prompts, questions, or tasks. Direct each table to draw a card at random and discuss it or complete the task, then repeat with another card as they're ready.
   - *Benefits:* Diversifies topics being discussed. Groups who finish early remain engaged by moving on to another card.
   - Example 1:
   Workshop Topic = "Teams"
   Cards = Discussion Prompts
     - Card A: If your team were a children's toy, what would they be, and why?
     - Card B: What are five essential attributes of amazing teams?
     - Card C: Who's the best teammate you've ever worked with, and what made that person effective as a team member?
     - Card D: Create a definition of "team" (without using online resources).
     - Card E: What's one effective practice your team rocks at?
   - Example 2:
   Workshop Topic = iPad Training
   Cards = Non-Sequential Device Set-Up Tasks (with directions)

- Card A: Name your iPad.
- Card B: Choose your home screen design.
- Card C: Turn off your keyboard sounds.
- Card D: Set up your email app.
- Card E: Choose your AirDrop settings.
- Card F: Explore the Accessibility options.

7. **Fist to Five**
   - People vote with their hand: fist (zero) means disagree; five fingers means 100% agree.
   - After asking a question or sharing a prompt, the facilitator says "go," and everyone holds up their hand- fist to five. It's important everyone reveals their number at the same time, so no one is swayed by others' responses.
   - The facilitator can then read the room and ask follow-up questions.
     - "Looks like we're all at 4's and 5's... pretty close to consensus and don't need to spend tons of time wrestling with this."
     - "Kae, you have a two. Will you share your thoughts?"
     - "Joe, I see your three. Why not a two? ... What would make it a four?"
     - "Travis, you have a five. What are you most excited about?"

8. **Eight Brains to One: Group Definition Activity**
   - See directions in Part 4: *Start Strong.*

9. **Labels for Processing Content**
   - People won't agree with everything you say. There will be things they need to wrestle with, compare to their experiences, and ponder. You want that! When you give them time to process and discuss, provide a creative word-set for labelling as they are processing.
   - Examples:
     - Nods. Shakes. Light Bulbs. (agree, disagree, new idea)
     - Resonating. Rumbling.
     - Clicks. Clunks.

10. **String Webs**
    - Small groups stand in a circle and one person is given a skein of yarn or ball of string. The person holding the string shares their answer to the prompt. No one else is allowed to respond- no affirmations, questions, or discussion at this time.
    - Holding onto the end of the string, they toss the ball to someone else in the circle. The receiver shares their answer to the prompt, holds the string taut, and tosses it to the next receiver.
    - Visually, this creates a web among the group as they share ideas.

- *Benefits:* This gives every person in the group an opportunity to respond and share their thoughts.
- After the webs are created by the small groups, the facilitator can provide time for open discussion, or follow up with whole group questions, such as "What struck you from the ideas shared in your group?"
- *Optional:* If the prompt has a meaningful inverse question, then Round 2 can be the undoing of the web as they toss the ball in reverse.
    - As an example, if Round 1 is about "barriers to exhibiting empathy," then Round 2 might be about "benefits and strategies for exhibiting empathy."

Ways to Create Partners and Groups

1. **Animal-Number Cards**
    - *See a ready-to-print-and-cut card deck at PositiveStrategery.com.*
    - Everyone gets one card. Each has an animal on one side and a number on the other.
    - I use eight animals and six numbers. Each animal is printed six times with a different number on the back.
        - shark, seahorse, crab, octopus (water)
        - camel, owl, rabbit, rhino (land)
        - numbers: 2, 3, 4, 15, 16, 17
    - Ways to create partners or groups:

(Find someone who's the same, or find someone who's different.)

Animals:
- land and sea
- carnivores and herbivores
- animal starts with the same letter
- cute or terrifying (subjective; fun because they get to decide)

Numbers:
- same number
- at least 10 apart
- even or odd
- prime or composite

2. **Deck of Playing Cards**
   - Similar to Animal-Number cards; everyone gets a card and pairs/groups can be created with numbers, suits, or colors.

3. **Quadrant Partners**
   - Everyone creates a 2x2 grid. The trainer provides a category for each square, such as:
     - Salty, Sweet, Spicy, Sour
     - Summer, Fall, Winter, Spring

- At the beginning of the day, everyone finds someone who can be their partner for each square in the 2x2 grid. As an example, Sam and Max might put each other's name down for the "Salty" square, Sam and Eva might put each other down for the Sweet square, etc.

- Throughout the day, the trainer can say, "Find your Sweet partner and chat about the prompt on screen."

- *Insight*: If using in workshops less than a full day, this can feel a bit cheesy and forced. It lands better when used in multi-day large group events where they might meet up with a quadrant partner more than once.

4. **No-Prep Groupings**
   - *In the moment, on the fly ways to easily create groups*
   - **Simple Pairs:** Pair up with someone who's not at your table, you haven't yet talked to today, etc.
   - **Simple Groups:** Number Around the Room
     - Facilitator has people number-off around the room (1234, 1234, 1234, …), then get into groups with their number.

Leveling Up Discussions for Transformation

Learning that yields a transformed perspective is a journey. It typically begins with a disorienting dilemma, involves deep reflection and discussion, and ends with the new perspective integrated into one's life. Transformative learning often happens in real-life within community, but it can occur, at least in part, in a formal training setting.

As a trainer, incorporating a bold statement or disorienting dilemma can be powerful because people pay extra attention to things that are jarring- that don't fit their current understanding or expectations. People also tend to dig in and defend their current beliefs.

If your topic is one that may spark strong opinions and passion, keep in mind that participants need to feel psychologically safe to share differing perspectives without fear of repercussions. They likely need *structures* to help share the air time, actively listen, and support both internal and external processors. If you're aiming for participants to have a transformed perspective, your discussion facilitation skills are paramount.

Transformative Learning In Action

In a past role, I taught teachers how to use technology in creative ways with students. When the elementary schools in my district began to use iPads, we developed a highly engaging, experiential full-day workshop to support meaningful implementation.

When it came time to teach the kindergarten and first-grade teachers, we gained an unsettling insight: the majority were *highly* resistant to the concept of screens in their classrooms. Yikes! We no longer needed just an engaging workshop that explored tools and developed skills; we were aiming for a transformed perspective on the creative and educational power of iPads in early-childhood classrooms.

The redesign was a beautiful process. Our goal wasn't to tell them we were right. Our goal was to unearth their concerns, facilitate a rich discussion, and help them experience meaningful ways to integrate the tool into their classrooms without violating their beliefs and expertise as educators.

Early in the workshop, we presented a **disorienting dilemma**: two national organizations they highly respected both found value in using technology in early-childhood classrooms.

We provided the official "position statements" from both organizations. Participants used the First Word, Last Word protocol to structure their **reflection** and **discussion** about the position statements. WIthout us needing to tell them, they made distinctions between creativity and consumption tasks on iPads; they talked about quantity and quality of screen time; and they felt bolstered knowing that the role of technology was not to replace their incredible value as teachers.

Throughout the day, they explored creativity apps. They experienced, discussed, and designed many ways to **integrate** the iPads into their classrooms for creative student learning. To close the workshop, they curated their key takeaways into Paper Slides, a low-tech video creation activity useful in any grade level including early-childhood.

About one month later, one of the attending teachers sent me evidence of her **transformed perspective**: Paper Slide videos her first-grade students made, using their iPads to capture their learning.

Planning an engaging workshop is a lot of work. Planning a transformational one takes even more intentionality, patience, and humility… much more challenging and totally worth it.

If you're aiming for a transformed perspective, plan structures to support the process. Also keep in mind it's not all within your control. Everyone is on a journey.

Discussion & Grouping Strategies
RECAP

Strategies:

1. Think, Pair, Share
2. Station Rotations
3. Around the Table
4. Table-Top Texting
5. First Word, Last Word
6. Prompt Cards on Tables
7. Fist to Five
8. Eight Brains to One
9. Labels for Processing Content
10. String Webs

Part 8

Breaks & Movement

> "When the butt goes numb, the brain goes dumb."
>
> classic trainer adage

You have the power to prevent participants' restlessness and daydreaming. All it takes is frequent transitions, quick brain-breaks, and, you guessed it… movement.

Increasing blood flow and oxygen improves brain function. So for people to bring their best, they need movement and deep breathing. Movement improves attention and learning, but movement 'activities' can also feel cheesy if the facilitator doesn't tee them up well. Be intentional to get people up and moving; do so in a way that works for your style *and* the participants.

The Best Energizer

Paper Rock Scissors: "Champions & Cheerleaders"

One of my fondest training memories is facilitating this at a multi-day event for two hundred new teachers. Picture it... Despite the timing being after lunch, *every* person is up and moving, and the energy in the room is incredible. In less than five minutes, two teachers are facing off for the final round of paper-rock-scissors, each backed by 99 other teachers wildly chanting their name. The uproar of encouragement gave me goosebumps.

The underlying message: Even when we 'lose,' our goal is to intentionally cheer others on.

A few weeks later, an elementary teacher sent me a video of her young students cheering each other on as the final two champions faced off in her classroom the first week of school. From hundreds of adults to 26 kids, this is my favorite energizer.

Directions:
- Everyone stands and finds a partner.
- Each time they find a partner, they must *first* learn their name, and *then* play paper-rock-scissors; best of three wins.

- **Winners (champions)** immediately find another partner who is also a "winner" (won their previous match)

- **Losers (cheerleaders)** become the winner's vocal cheerleader, following behind them and audibly cheering them on using their name.

- Every time someone loses a match, they, along *with all their current cheerleaders*, become cheerleaders for the person who won that match.

- Even with 100+ people, in under five minutes, you'll have the final two winners facing off, *each backed by half the room cheering them on!*

Strategies With Movement

1. **"Stand Up And…"**
    - Every so often, have people **stand up** as they talk to a partner or in small groups, instead of sitting at their tables. Get their blood moving.

    - The **Station Rotations** strategy is a more structured version of this concept. (See Part 7: *Discussions & Groups*).

    - *Insight:* People are sometimes hesitant to physically stand up when they're talking to people who are already at their table. Explain the *reason* for having them stand and chat (to re-engage their brains), and use a Grouping Strategy from the previous chapter.

2. **Agreement Circle - Step In, Step Out**
   - One person steps in and responds to the prompt. Those who agree, step in. Everyone then steps back and the next person steps in and responds.
   - Example Prompts:
     - "One thing I'm most excited about with this new tool is…"
     - "A challenge I've faced related to today's learning topic is…"
     - "Of this list of quotes, the one that resonates with me most is…"

3. **Continuum**
   - Participants stand on an invisible line in the room, where they think they fit based on facilitator-provided prompts.
   - Example Prompts:
     - How You Prefer to Vacation *End Points:* rest; no plans … itinerary; go-go-go
     - How You Prefer to Take Notes *End Points:* paper … digital
     - Experience Level with Today's Topic *End Points:* novice … expert

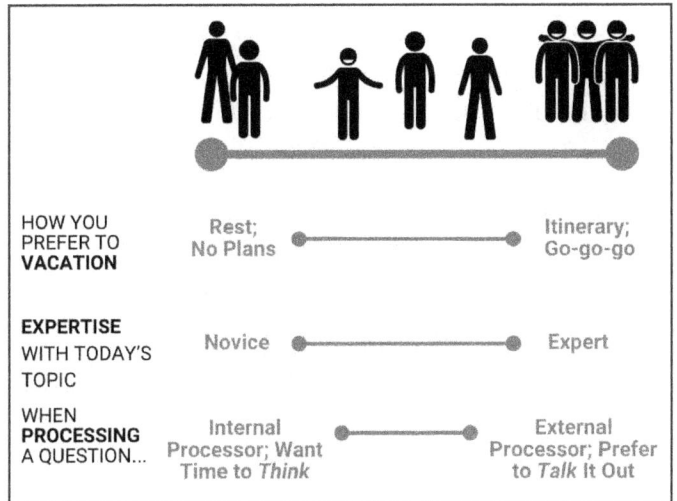

- Benefits:
    - Gets learners moving *and* people like taking a stand based on their opinions.
    - Allows them to see differences in the room.
    - Allows the facilitator to read the room and acknowledge where they're at.

- PRO TIPS
    - It's okay to start with a couple silly ones to warm up; however, *mostly* use prompts that connect to the workshop topic.
    - Help learners be reflective and pay attention to others, not just themselves.
    - If it's a large group, consider *curving* the imaginary line into more of a U-shape, so they can all see each other once they plant their feet.

4. **Unique Me Cards**
   - **Prep:** At the beginning of the event, participants create a top-secret notecard with three things that are true about them, each item is progressively more *unique*:
     1. something they think *many* others in the room have in common with them
     2. something that *a few* in the room might have in common with them
     3. something they think *no one* in the room will have in common with them (unique)
   - The cards are given to you, the facilitator.
   - Randomly throughout the day, have everyone stand for a quick stretch and brain break. Pick a card.
     - Say, *"**Stay standing if this is true of you...**"* then read the first item on the card.
     - After some people sit down, say *"**Of those still standing, remain standing if...**"* and read the second item on the card.
     - After more people sit down, repeat with the last item.
   - Let the person standing (the card creator) share a quick insight about their unique item. Then start over and repeat with one more card, or move on with the workshop.

- You can do the activity multiple times in a half-day session. You won't use most of the cards- that's okay!

- Benefits:
    - Easily used at any time during the workshop; takes less than a minute.
    - Gets everyone up, increasing blood flow and oxygen, so they're fresh and bring their best to the next section of the workshop.
    - Everyone learns something interesting about the card creator.

Alternative Version: 2 Truths and a Dream

- An improved twist on 2 Truths and a *Lie*.

- Each person comes up with two things that are true about them, and one dream or aspiration they have.

- As a version of **Unique Me Cards**, everyone writes theirs on a card at the beginning. When a transition or quick brain break is needed, everyone stands up. The facilitator picks a card and reads all three from a card, pauses for dramatic effect, then asks only the card creator to remain standing.

- Now that everyone knows whose card it is, they will guess which of the three they think is the "dream." The facilitator re-reads each item, one at a time. People stand for the one they think is the "dream."

5. **Pipe Cleaners on Tables**
   - *Cheap and disposable!*
   - **Use 1:** Place on tables as optional fidgets/toys. Doing something with your hands, such as drawing or creating a pipe cleaner shape, can improve focus.
     - Let people know they are welcome to play with them as they listen and learn. If you don't say this, many will assume they are for a specific activity and off-limits.
   - **Use 2:** They can be used in a specific activity, such as having learners use a pipe cleaner to create a symbol that represents something they've learned in the session. (This is art; it's very open to interpretation.) After 90 seconds to create, have them give it to a partner and explain the reasoning behind their creation.

Formal Breaks

As a general guideline, aim to give participants an official, unfacilitated 5-10 minute break about every 90 minutes. *You* may not need it as a trainer (you're up, moving, and talking), but *they* need it. They need time to check emails, zone out, and take care of self and work.

Launch the Break

- Put a countdown **timer** on screen.
- **Communicate** that everyone should be back and ready when the timer goes off. Remember it's your responsibility to articulate clear expectations, not assume it's common sense or courtesy.
- **Encourage them to move** around during the break, even if it's just standing while they chat, or walking in the hallway. (Not everyone will do it, and that's okay.)

Return from Break

- Captivate and re-engage them with something better than, "Alright everyone, it's time to keep rolling." Play a song or video clip, or have an activity like a Word Unscramble on screen.

- *Insight:* The struggle to recall something we've learned helps solidify that learning. Try one of these when coming back from a break:

    - "Tell your partner what you remember from this morning's session?"

    - "Write down one thing you commit to doing from the previous section. Try not to look at your notes."

From energizers to movement strategies to formal breaks, remember: **movement is magic.**

Breaks & Movement Strategies
RECAP

Strategies:

1. Stand Up And…

2. Agreement Circle - Step In, Step Out

3. Continuum

4. Unique Me Cards

5. Pipe Cleaners on Tables

Part 9

Improv Games With Meaning

Improv (improvisational theater) isn't just about having a great funny bone. Improv requires courage, teamwork, trust, creativity, listening, timing, reading people and situations, being willing to lead, and being able to follow. Improv games are a perfect vessel for cultivating these qualities even in settings outside the theater... like your workshops!

A few years ago, I had the privilege to meet **Eric Epperson**, an executive-level leader and improv guru. In addition to his nonprofit leadership work, Eric serves as a conference emcee and leads workshops using exercises commonly found in a comedy improv class. As attendees participate, amidst the laughter, Eric helps them make connections to leadership, teamwork, and communication.

When I met Eric for coffee, I asked him to share some of his go-to games and specifically- their deeper takeaways.

With a smile and generous spirit, he shared the six below, and gave me permission to pass them on to you.

Improv games can have a deep meaning connected to your topic. As an exceptional trainer, you're not using these as goofy icebreakers. You're using the ones packed with meaning.

PRO TIPS for *Facilitating* Improv Games

Before you learn the games, let's get you ready to *facilitate* them like a pro.

1. Help develop psychological safety. Let the group know it's okay to fail and be silly. Throughout the experience, remind them it's about learning and having fun, not about being right.

2. Give clear directions about how to play the game. Do a quick demonstration. Specify "who goes first" and "clockwise." (See Part 7: *Discussions & Groups*.) This helps them focus on the game without having to think about those logistics.

3. Plan time for post-game discussion.

    A. "What are your takeaways? What did you learn?"

    B. "What connections to real life or deeper meaning might the experience represent?"

C. As needed, add to their answers. Share the takeaway you want to be sure they get, such as those listed in each game's description in this chapter.

D. Lead a "now what?" discussion on the application. "What does it look like to incorporate that message into your work or life?" Ask them for practical examples.

MEANINGFUL IMPROV GAMES

1. WORD ASSOCIATION

The Gist:

When it's your turn, say a word you associate with the previous word spoken. Don't think about it; just say it.

Examples:

- Light → Dark → Chocolate → Ice Cream → Summer → Sunshine → Ray → Bradbury
- Dog → Fire Hydrant → Water → Ice → Freezer → Burn → Spy → Magnifying Glass

How to Play:

- Create small groups, typically 5-8 people per group.
- Give direction guidance (e.g. clockwise) and "who goes first" guidance.

- Tell them:
    - You must say your word quickly.
    - There are no right or wrong answers/words.
- Person 1 starts by saying any appropriate word.
- Person 2 says any word that comes to mind when they hear Person 1's word.
- Person 3 says any word that comes to mind when they hear Person 2's word. ...and so on.

The Common Takeaways:

- Don't overthink it.
- It's okay to mess up.
- There's not always a perfect or right answer.
- Sometimes wanting to be right or look smart can hold us back.

2. **PASS THE APPLAUSE, A.K.A. SYNCHRO-CLAP**

The Gist:

A single clap/applause is passed around the perimeter of a circle but can only be passed if the two people clapping do so at exactly the same time.

How to Play:

- Create small groups, typically 5-8 people per group.
- Give direction guidance (e.g. clockwise) and "who goes first" guidance.

- Person 1 turns to the neighbor on their left, who we'll call Person 2. Person 1 initiates a clap gesture, and Person 2 must clap at the exact same time as Person 1.
  - If they are *not* in unison, they must try again until they get the timing perfectly in sync.
- Once they clap in unison, Person 2 turns to their left and passes the clap/applause to the next person. ... and so on.
- *Noteworthy:*
  - Some groups or pairs will really struggle to clap in sync. Others will get into a rhythm and start flying around the circle.
- Options/Variations for a more complex Round 2:
  - Have them go the opposite direction around the circle.
  - Add a rule that *double-clapping* reverses the direction the applause is being passed around the circle. Each person may choose whether to clap once or twice.
  - Let them pass the applause to anyone at any time, not just around the circle.
  - Start with two different people passing a clap/applause within the same circle.

Common Takeaways:

- Getting into a rhythm can be tough and slow. Once you do, things flow somewhat effortlessly.

- When the goal is clear, in this case *rhythm*, people collaborate instead of compete.

- Looking at people's eyes during the game is often more productive than looking at their hands. Prioritize *people and connection*, not just tasks.

> **PRO TIP** **Learn from my mistake-**
>
> - Online, you may see this game called "Pass the Clap." In a professional workshop, that title is not ideal because "the clap" is also slang for a sexually transmitted disease. So as you facilitate the exercise, you find yourself saying: "Okay, it's time to Pass the Clap." … "See if you can Pass the Clap faster!" … "Way to go- we're all Passing the Clap now!" Can you hear it? Yikes. I made this mistake with a group of 25 emerging leaders. Some didn't make the connection but others couldn't stop chuckling. I was in the group that didn't make the connection until after I'd facilitated the activity… embarrassing *and* hilarious. I now call the game "Pass the ***Applause***."

3. YES AND BIKE

The Gist:

People add items to an imaginary bike that belongs to a group. Before adding something new, they first affirm the items previously added.

How to Play:

- Small group stands in a circle.
- Tell them they are building an imaginary bike together.
- The first person holds their hands in the air as if holding the handlebars of a bicycle. They say: "This is **our** bike, and it has _____." Tell them to be creative- anything goes. (You don't need to give them examples, but to help you envision the concept, they might end up adding things like a basket, a rusty bell that doesn't work, or wings that make it fly.)
- The second person goes, holding the imaginary handlebars. They say, "This is **our** bike, and it has _____ *and* _____." They first repeat all the previous items that have been added to the bike before adding their new item.
- Repeat around the circle until time is called.
- Have each group nominate a speaker who will share their bike with the room, holding the handlebars and saying: "This is **our** bike, and it has _____."

Common Takeaways:

- Let go. You don't *own* the bike.
- We're stronger with many ideas. Anyone can describe a creative bike, but individually they would never come up with what the *group* creates together.

- There's value in affirmations, such as simply acknowledging the previous idea before sharing a new one.
- Visualization and repetition are useful tools for memory.

4. COUNT TO TWENTY

The Gist:

A group counts to 20 by having one person say a number at any given time. Eyes are closed and there's no specific speaking order.

How to Play:

- Standing up, small groups form a circle. Each person puts their hands on their neighbors' shoulders. Everyone closes their eyes.
- The Goal: Count to 20 as a group.
- The Rules:
    1. No one speaks at the same time.
    2. No consecutive speakers. This means when someone says a number, then the person on their right and their left cannot be the ones who say the next number.
- If either rule is broken, the group must start over.

Common Takeaways:

- Don't hesitate or overthink it.

- Sometimes taking action is better than being paralyzed. Even if you fail, you're moving forward and learning.
- You can only do so much; you can't do it all.
- We win or lose *together*.

5. CARDS 1-100

The Gist:

Everyone receives a random numbered card. The group must play their cards in sequence without overtly communicating.

How to Play:

- Facilitator provides groups with a deck of 100 cards, numbered 1 through 100.
- Everyone takes one card from the deck.
- The group must play their cards in sequence, lowest first, highest last, without talking making gestures, or knowing anyone else's card.
- For example: If Bob plays his 7 card, Jane might pause then play her 15, hoping everyone else's card is above 15. She might be right, or maybe Jo was holding a 13 and just didn't play fast enough.
- If/When a mistake is made, all cards are returned to the deck, new cards are drawn, and the group immediately tries again.

- If they complete the task, in the second round, everyone takes *two* cards. Same rules apply.

Common Takeaways:
- it's okay to fail.
- *Trying* despite the unknown is better than being frozen by fear of being wrong.

6. SPACE WALK

The Gist:

People use their feet/gait to demonstrate different emotions.

How to Play:
- Everyone starts walking around a spacious room. The facilitator provides an emotion word, and they all have to *walk it out* with their feet.
- Facilitator reminds them: "Don't think. *Feel*."
- Repeat with different emotion words.
- *Bonus:* Notice and have them observe the difference between nuanced, seemingly similar emotion words, such as "angry," "annoyed," and "frustrated."

Common Takeaways:
- Much of communication is nonverbal.
- How we feel affects how we act and show up.

- Recognizing how you feel is important for regulating your emotions.
- How we express our emotions can vary person to person.

Your clear directions and control of the room (i.e. ability to bring them back for discussion) are essential for these improv games to go well. Since I'm not an improv guru or a comedian, I'm always a bit nervous when I use one of these; yet, when I follow the Pro Tips at the beginning of this chapter, the experience is wildly engaging.

Plan well, be confident, and try a *meaningful* improv game to enhance learning in your workshop.

Improv Games With Meaning
RECAP

Games

1. Word Association
2. Pass the Applause
3. Yes And Bike
4. Count to Twenty
5. Cards 1-100
6. Space Walk

Part 10

Call Backs & Attention Signals

Inevitably there will be a time during your workshop when you need to get participants' attention and bring them back together from partner chats, table discussions, and lively group activities. With a small group, this is easy and conversational. For larger groups, you need a strategy. Without an attention signal or call back strategy, you may end up repeatedly yelling, "Okay come back now" or begin moving on while some participants are still engaged in their conversations... *awkward.*

Exceptional trainers don't talk over people, compete with their conversations, or leave them behind. You want to bring learners back and facilitate the pace in a respectful, effective way.

Elementary school teachers are pros at call backs. They choose a few that work for their style, practice them with students, and reuse them all year long.

Call Back (auditory) & Attention Signal (visual)

1. **Slow Countdown from Five**
   - Raises your hand in the air and say, "We're coming back together in 5... 4..."
   - Counting *slowly* is important; the goal is to give them time to quickly finish their conversation.

2. **Silent Hand Raise**
   - *my personal favorite when facilitating large groups*
   - Proactively teach participants to raise their hand when they see yours raised. This is an acknowledgement that they see you and a visual signal to their peers. They can finish their conversation but won't start a new one.
   - When it's time to bring them back, raise your hand high as you walk around the room.
   - Even a large room is usually silent and ready to move on within two minutes.

3. **Call & Response**
   - A favorite of elementary teachers, this call back style can feel too cutesy or condescending for adults. If you try a call-and-response, tee it up well and make sure you can build buy-in for it.

   Examples:
   - "Ready to rock? ... Ready to roll!"

- "Shark bait ... ooo ha ha" (*Finding Nemo*)
- "If you can hear me, clap once. If you can hear me, clap twice." (pause, repeat, pause, repeat)

4. **Stand in a Specific Spot**
   - Proactively teach participants that the only time you'll stand on that chair or stage, or in that particular front corner, is when you're signaling to them it's time to move on.

5. **Chime or Sound**
   - Products exist specifically for teachers and trainers to purchase, or you may find a sound online you can play/download.

6. **Break Into Song**
   - I've only seen this used once by a hilarious and eccentric trainer. It worked perfectly, but only because it fit her authentic style.

> **PRO TIP** **Proactively explain the signal you'll use.**
>
> Early in the workshop, go over logistics and the call back or attention signal you will use. Teach, model, and even do a quick practice at the start of the workshop. If you wait until everyone is engrossed in your first interesting discussion prompt, then attempt to grab their attention with a signal they aren't familiar with, it will be awkward and ineffective.

Explain your attention signal or call back, how it will work, and *why* you're using it. Without the *why*, some people may feel like the strategy is condescending or unnecessary. I say something like this:

"There will be times I need to bring everyone back from an engaging activity. I don't want to interrupt your great conversations, yet part of my role is to keep us moving. In order to do this, I'm going to use _____ as a signal that it's time to come back together." (Then I model it or have them practice.)

If it's a large group, I have them practice by talking to their neighbor about weekend plans for 60 seconds, just so they can experience how it will work to be brought back with the signal.

Call Backs and Attention Signal Strategies
RECAP

Strategies

1. Slow Countdown from Five
2. Silent Hand Raise
3. Call-and-Response
4. Stand in a Specific Spot
5. Chime or Sound
6. Break Into Song

Part 11

Choose Your Words

Exceptional trainers choose their words intentionally.

WORTHY PHRASES

Invite Participation & Honor Autonomy

- "If you're willing…"
- "I'd like to invite you to…"
- "Play or pass?"
    - Example: "As we go around, you can *Play or Pass*. I hope you're willing to *play* each time so we all learn from each other. I will also respect if you're not yet ready to share something."

Responding to Their Responses

Keep in mind: You don't need to elaborate on or one-up each shared comment.

- "Thank you for sharing."

- "Thank you for being bold and going first."
- "Will you elaborate on that?"
- "Tell us more…"
- "Great, we've got one experience/idea. Let's get some more. Who else?" or "What else?"

Articulate Clear Expectations

Specificity is key.

- "What can I clarify?"
- "What's hazy or unclear?"
- "What questions do you have?"
- "To ensure the directions are clear, will someone volunteer to restate the directions in their own words?"
- "Partner A, explain the directions to Partner B." (If anyone furrows their brow and you hear confused "*Ums*," then clarity is needed.)
- "Do _____, **which looks like…**"
    - *Example:* "As you share your answer around the circle, *this looks like* giving the headline (just a phrase or sentence), not the whole story (paragraphs)."

- *Example:* "Let's take a 10 minute break. *This looks like* taking care of anything you need to, getting up and moving, and committing to be back and ready to rock as soon as the timer goes off."

- "Do _____ *...by doing...*"

  - *Example:* "Please clean up before you leave *by* putting the supplies back in the boxes, cleaning up your trash, and pushing your chairs in."

Keep Things Moving

Specifically when a comment or group conversation begins to derail the focus.

- "This is an interesting topic (or conversation). Being mindful of the time we have and our goals for this workshop, I'm going to keep us moving."

- "This has the potential for a rich discussion. In order to keep us focused on our topic and learning goals, we're going to shift gears."

- "Will you write that on a sticky note and put it on our thought-catcher poster as a topic for future discussion?"

BANNED PHRASES

Quick List

Exceptional trainers do not say:

- "Do you have any questions?"
- "I'll treat you like adults." / "You're adults, so…"
- "I know it's early / Monday / after-lunch / not your choice to be here," *etc.*
- "We're going to talk about…" *or* "I'm going to talk to you about…" *or* "I'm going to tell you a story…"
- "We'll come back to that." *or* " We're going to talk about that later."
- "Does that make sense?" or "Get it?"
- "We all love technology until it doesn't work, right?"
- "If no one volunteers, I WILL call on someone."
- "Ok, on to the next."
- "Honestly, this is my favorite part."
- *jargon and acronyms*
- *gimmicky references to the COVID pandemic*
- *and…*(insert **your** filler word/phrase here)

Banned Phrases Explained

- **"Do you have any questions?"**
  - *Why not?* It's a closed, yes/no question, often resulting in a conversation-ending "no."
  - *Better Phrasing:*
    - ✓ "What questions do you have?"
    - ✓ "If you had to ask one question, what would it be?"

- **"I'll treat you like adults." / "You're adults, so…"**
  - *Why not?* It implies you considered the possibility of treating them as children; it's off putting and condescending.

- **"I know it's early / Monday / after-lunch / not your choice to be here,"** etc.
  - *Why not?* You're planting seeds of negativity. You're giving participants an excuse for low energy. Remember, your energy and tone are contagious.
  - *Better Phrasing:*
    - ✓ "It's early and you all are here! This is going to be amazing!" (Or don't mention that it's early at all, just be excited they're here!)
    - ✓ "Since it's after lunch, let's stand up for this next activity and keep our bodies and minds active." *If it's a mandated training-*

✓ "Your company/organization is so cool. They think highly of you all, and they value giving you protected time to learn *together*."

- **"We're going to talk about…"** *also not* "I'm going to talk to you about…" *also not* "I'm going to tell you a story…"

  - *Why not?* This is one of my pet peeves. A comedian doesn't start by saying "I'm going to tell you some jokes." There's no need to state that you're *going to* tell a story.

  - *Better Phrasing:* Just like a comedian launches right into the joke, get right to it! Dive right into the *enrapturing hook* of your topic or story. Remember, *start strong*.

- **"We'll come back to that."**
Also not "We're going to talk about that later."

  - *Why not?* Most often, this phrase is said when you accidentally let your stream of consciousness run, and you slip into a topic you plan to cover later in the talk or workshop. This comes across as awkward and unprepared. The learners are thinking, 'Why did you bring it up then?' or 'Why can't we talk about that now?'

  - *Better Phrasing:* Embrace the power in the pause and keep yourself from steering the group off course if you're not willing to go there. If a *participant* comment is the culprit, try something like:

✓ "Joe, thanks for bringing that up. Before we go there, let's make sure we've got our current topic wrapped up."

- **"Does that make sense?"** *or* **"Get it?"**

  - *Why not?* People hardly ever say "no" to this, even if they *are* actually lost. These are questions you ask to boost your ego, not genuinely check for understanding.

  - *Better Phrasing:*
    - ✓ "What questions do you have?"
    - ✓ "Is someone willing to rephrase this in their own words, so we make sure we're all on the same page?"

- **Jargon and Acronyms**

  - *Why Not?* You believe people are smart. You want them to feel valued and to learn. You don't want them to get lost or feel stupid.

  - *Better Phrasing:* Use simple language that's accessible to everyone. When you're going to continually use an acronym, explain it in full the first time.

- **Gimmicky references to the COVID pandemic**, such as, "We used to do ABC, until something weird happened in 2020… can't remember what it was."

  - *Why not?* It's corny and overused. You want to be fresh and genuine.

- *Better Phrasing:* If you want to talk about something pivotal from that time, do it with sincerity.

- **"We all love technology until it doesn't work, right?"**

  - *Why not?* Don't blame the tech when there is a tech issue. It shows you're thrown-off and annoyed.

  - *Better Phrasing:* Be prepared with a meaningful reflection or discussion question that, if needed, you can ask participants to write about or discuss. Be ready to engage them on the learning topic while the issue is being resolved behind the scenes.

- **"If no one volunteers, I WILL call on someone."**

  - *Why not?* Great trainers and speakers never condescend or threaten.

  - *Better Phrasing:*

    - ✓ "I'm hoping for 2 courageous people willing to share, *so that* we can all grow from other perspectives and insights."

    - ✓ "You don't have to share your own idea. Did anyone *hear* something interesting from someone else during your table discussion?"

    - ✓ "I'm working on giving people time to have thoughtful answers. Take a moment to think; let me know when you're ready to share."

✓ See phrases under the *Invite Participation & Honor Autonomy* section at the beginning of this chapter.

  ✓ Be sure your question/prompt is open-ended and thought-provoking.

  ✓ Embrace the silence.

Also Avoid Filler and Empty Words

- **"Ok, on to the next."**
- **"Honestly, this is my favorite part."** (implies the rest is not as good)
- **"Um"**
- **"You know."**
- **"[insert YOUR filler word or phrase here]**
    - It's common to have filler words without realizing it. One colleague I know used to say "'kay" (short for "okay") after every few sentences. Another speaker I know used to say "Hey guys…" at least 15 times in a session.
    - Video yourself or ask a radically candid friend to help you identify your filler words. It will be uncomfortable to uncover them. It will also be *totally worth it*. You'll thank me later.

Exceptional trainers choose their words. Start by identifying a worthy phrase you will implement consistently, and a banned phrase you commit to eradicating.

Part 12

Tips for Facilitating a Virtual Training

When I was tasked with facilitating my first virtual workshop, anxiety bubbled up, primarily because I knew my vision disability would create some challenges navigating the platform and reading participant names. Once I took a breath, I dove into studying and practicing how to be exceptional at facilitating virtual learning. Here's what I learned:

1. **Prepare!**

There are several different virtual presentation and video conferencing platforms. Whichever one you use, commit time to explore and master it before you go live. Also be sure all updates are installed. There's nothing worse than having to restart your computer minutes before your session is scheduled to begin.

2. **Log in on a *second device.* Give that participant the name "Presenter Slides."**

When you present slides full-screen, you (the presenter) lose sight of participants, at least in the platform I was using. If you have a second device, you can present the slides on one, and keep participants' faces on screen on the other device. This also allows you to, if needed, look something up in a new tab without having to stop presenting your slides.

3. **Proactively communicate clear and direct expectations.**

Just like for in-person workshops, talking through logistics and expectations at the beginning makes a huge difference Examples:
- "Let's use Chat minimally and for these reasons…"
- "After we talk about logistics I'm going to ask you to turn on your camera even if you're having a bad hair day *because…*"
- "To maximize your visuals on screen, I recommend you use Gallery View and slide the divider bar sideways to make the presented screen-shared slides smaller."

4. **Help people feel connected and seen.**
- *Otherwise, this could have just been a video.*
- Use their names throughout the session.

- Make time for introductions and connections. (This doesn't have to take long.)
  - Use the Chat, breakout rooms, or go live around the screen. I like to have the person who's speaking call on the next person. This requires everyone to pay attention and eliminates the need for *me* to call on people.
  - Provide a simple, interesting question they can answer as part of their intro.
  - Model by going first, especially if you want to model brevity.

5. **Embrace the silence after you ask a question.**

Giving participants 'wait/think time' is *always* wildly important, but *even more so in a virtual environment*. If you provide a great prompt and want participants to engage, then they need time to think AND time to muster the courage to unmute and speak on camera. As the facilitator, become comfortable with 30+ seconds of silence after the prompt, as well as after someone answers, to give space for "What else? / Who else?".

6. **Say "go" to post in the Chat.**

When you have people post their answer in the Chat, tell them to wait until you say "3-2-1-Go" before they *post*. This gives everyone time to think without getting distracted by the first posts. And the flood of posts all at once creates a great energy.

7. **Provide breaks.**

Staring at a screen is draining. Depending on the duration of your session, plan for camera-off breaks. Encourage everyone to move and get away from their device during that time. Put the countdown timer on screen. Before they depart, give clear expectations.

Example:
- "There's a timer on-screen. If you're stepping away, (and I hope you are!), please set a timer on your phone. Commit to being back on time, so we're not awkwardly waiting or leaving behind someone who returns late."

8. **If you use small group discussions (breakout rooms), provide thoughtful questions/prompts.**

Ensure the prompt is interesting, clear, and open-ended. Spark meaningful conversation. Post the prompt in the Chat so participants can see it while in the breakout room.

9. **Utilize a co-facilitator or nominate a "Chat leader."**

When possible, have a co-facilitator whose primary purpose is to monitor and moderate the Chat. They'll vocalize noteworthy questions or comments they see, and post useful resource links as they're mentioned in the training. This frees you up to speak and facilitate conversations without needing to simultaneously read and type.

10. Make it exceptional!

Even though the environment is virtual, the beliefs and radically simple strategies in this book still apply. Don't default to a dull one-sided presentation just because it's online. Start strong, end strong, and engage the learners in meaningful ways.

Part 13

Rad Simple Ways to Keep Improving

Greatness requires practice, continually sharpening your skills. The tips in this section are simple and the ideas are easy... so easy that they are often overlooked. The radical part of *radically simple ideas* happens when you live them out.

1. **Practice, Practice, Practice**
   - Studying, planning, and reflecting on experiences is important and useful. Becoming exceptional also requires *doing*. Lots and lots of *doing*.

   - One great way to practice is by submitting session proposals for local conferences. You'll likely donate your time (do it for free), but it's worth it to *practice* while helping others learn. And as a bonus, you can observe other speakers' sessions too.

2. **Use Your *Greatness Elements* and *Pet Peeves***
   - Convert your lists from the opening chapter in this book into your formal preparation checklist.

3. **Record Yourself**
   - It may be painful to watch, but it's also one of the most powerful tools for growth. You'll see your strengths, your quirks, and your areas that need improvement.
   - This doesn't have to be fancy or expensive. There are great budget-friendly options for phone tripods and wireless mics.
   - Keep in mind, you don't need to fix everything all at once. Have something specific you're watching for, such as a strong start and close, your filler words, or your body language. Try using a rubric or checklist to make the observations objective. Or, look for both of these:
     - What 1-2 things were great?
     - What 1-2 things would make it even better next time?

4. **Seek Feedback Strategically**
   - **Ask a friend, colleague, or mentor** to observe you for the specific purpose of giving feedback. Give them one or two *specific* things you'd like them to watch for.

- **Be wary of *conversationally* asking *participants* for feedback on your delivery.** Chatting with people after my workshops, I used to ask for feedback on how the session went. It was never fruitful- people just shrugged or said nice things. This was actually pretty selfish because I was shifting their minds away from the *learning* and toward *me*. When chatting after the session, you might instead ask: "What's the one thing you think you'll remember six months from now?" or "What's the one thing you're excited to put into practice?" This genuinely provokes their reflection while giving you insight on what was most impactful.

- **Use feedback surveys with participants.** If you use digital feedback surveys at the end of a session or event, be sure to give participants five minutes to complete the evaluation *within the time allocated for your session*. This honors their time, as well as significantly increases the participation rate compared to emailing a survey afterward.

  > **PRO TIPS**
  > - Keep your feedback survey simple and concise.
  > - Only ask questions that will give you *actionable* insight.
  > - Have them complete the survey *before facilitating* the closing activity.

- **Sample Feedback-Survey Questions**
    1. On a scale of 1-4, how likely are you to recommend this session to someone who's very similar to yourself? (Use an even number; no middle option.)
    2. What was your ONE favorite, most memorable part that you'll remember six months from now? a story, phrase, stat, tip, etc.
    3. Help improve the next iteration of this workshop or speech. What was ONE lull, one thing that didn't pop, or one recommendation you have for improving the content or delivery? "It would be even better next time if…"
    4. What's ONE thing you're going to do as a result of this learning event?

5. **Study the Science of Learning**

"The science of learning" is an integrated field of study, incorporating neuroscience, education, and psychology (cognitive, behavioral, and developmental). Knowing more about it will help you design your training for maximum learning.

A Few Radically Simple Insights

- Taking in new information (called "encoding") is most effective when the new knowledge or learning experience is **multi-faceted** such as: emotional, uses your senses, and is represented in multiple formats (visual cues, reading text, etc.).

- As we **sleep**, learning moves from short-term memory to long-term memory (called "consolidation"). Our mind fills in the gaps in the learning by connecting it to our past experiences and knowledge.

- **Effort** is required for lasting learning. This is true both in the initial phase when exposed to new information, and in the retrieval phase when struggling to pull the learning from long-term memory to conscious working memory.

- **Effortful retrieval**, the uncomfortable moments when we are looking for but can't yet remember something, is a *productive* struggle.

- **Spaced practice** over time, rather than mass practice in one sitting, strengthens the learning as it moves back and forth between long-term and short-term memory.

Consider deepening your expertise by exploring additional learning science concepts, such as:

- Short Term Memory
- Long Term Memory
- Working Memory
- Cognitive Load
- Interleaving
- Repetition
- Psychological Safety
- Zone of Proximal Development
- Learning Transfer
- Durable Learning

6. **Observe to Learn**
   - *Participate* in workshops and conferences. Take notes and learn not only the content but also from the trainer or speaker's style. Notice and analyze specific things like how they open, transition, pause, ask questions, tell stories, and close.
   - Add to your Greatness Elements and Pet Peeves lists. Keep gathering reusable strategies- there are so many great ones out there! Write them down in a place you'll never lose them, like in this book. The last few pages are for you.

7. **Be Radical!**
   - Keep this book handy, because you don't just *like* the ideas... you *implement* them. Continually revisit it to refresh your mindset, plan strategically, and incorporate radically simple strategies to make your training exceptional.

If you feel a stirring
to spur growth in others
through training and speaking-
lean into it.

Commit to becoming **exceptional**
through practice, feedback, and
implementing the radically simple
beliefs and strategies
in this book.

There are people in the world
who need what you have to teach.
Lead them well.

Credits & Bonus Resources

Workshop, Training, & Speaking

Greatness Elements

The best ones are… have… do…

My Workshop & Speaker

Pet Peeves

So instead I'll do…

More Insights & Strategies

Add to this page as you continually gather even more ways to be exceptional and help others grow…

Strategy, Phrase, or Insight	*Use & Impact*

Inspiration & Credits

I could not have written this book without the insightful feedback and continual support from my favorite person, my husband and partner in both business and life, Joe Shaw. Did you know Joe and I are co-writing the next *Radically Simple* book together, all about reusable questions for various contexts? I can't wait for you to read it!

Many thanks to Janet Goldstein who advised me to write my "starter book," and to Travis, Deb, and Deanna for your book preview feedback.

The global community of trainers and speakers is generous- we're continually sharing and gleaning ideas from one another. This makes it tough to trace the *original* creator of training strategies, so here I'll credit those who were *my* introduction to some concepts in this book:

- Goose Leadership Analogy/Story - Angela Grunewald and Sheila Stinnett
- "Be the Hope" - Mark Madewell
- Metaphor Image Cards (as affirmations for team members) - Kerri Price via LinkedIn
- String Maps - April Kitchen
- Group Anthem - "I am, I believe, I will…" - Nate Folan and Chad Littlefield
- The Phone Call - Heather Italiano

- Fist to Five - Travis Hardin and Justin Self
- String Webs - Tessa Kampen
- Unique Me Cards - Amy Speidel
- 2 Truths & 1 Dream - Elizabeth Souder

Let's strive to be like these cool people-
share generously, borrow often, and give as much as you get.

Help Other Trainers Grow

Two ways you can help spread the word about this radically simple guide, so more and more trainings become exceptional -

1. Share what you're learning and implementing. **Post favorite quotes and strategies** and mention the book. #RadicallySimple

2. **Write a review** (on Amazon, Goodreads, or your favorite book site). Honest reviews from real people like you can make a big difference.

So glad you're a part of the generous community of collaborative, *exceptional* trainers!

BONUS RESOURCES

PositiveStrategery.com

- Animal-Number Cards
- Image Metaphor Cards
- Sample Slides for Activities
- Plan Like A Pro
  One-Page Checklist

About The Author

Tami Shaw is a dynamic keynote speaker and workshop facilitator, passionate about using radically simple ideas to evoke empathy, provoke strategic thinking, and develop extraordinary communicators. Tami has spent her career as a people-development expert with nearly two decades focused on training, communications, and organizational systems design.

Through their company Positive Strateg*ery*, Tami and her husband Joe provide speaking, training, and consulting that helps organizations, leaders, and teams gain clarity and maximize their impact.

Tami has had what she calls a series of dream jobs, including teaching 8th-grade math in Arizona, innovating as the head of professional development in Oklahoma's third-largest public school district, and serving companies in her community with affordable training through the local career-tech center.

Tami is a Working Genius Certified Facilitator with a Bachelor's in English Education and a Master's in Talent Development. To spark a light-up conversation with Tami, bring up: strategic organizational design, training design, word choice, empathy, or... Trader Joe's.

Connect and follow Tami:

 @TamiShaw2614

 PositiveStrategery.com

www.ingramcontent.com/pod-product-compliance
Lightning Source LLC
Chambersburg PA
CBHW061649040426
42446CB00010B/1650